Contents

Words appearing in the text in bold, **like this**, are explained in the Glossary.

Who were the ancient Egyptians?

Long ago the **civilization** of ancient Egypt flourished on the banks of the River Nile, in the north of Africa. It was the world's first truly great civilization, and it lasted for over 3000 years. We can find out the fascinating story of its people and their achievements by studying the remains of buildings and tombs that survive to this day.

Egypt's mighty river

The River Nile was of great importance to the ancient Egyptians. When a famous **historian** from ancient Greece, a man called Herodotus, visited Egypt in the 400s BC he wrote: 'Egypt is the gift of the Nile'. This was a very wise thing to say. The Nile provided the people of Egypt with water for drinking and bathing. Its fish and **wildfowl** were caught for food, and it was the country's most important highway, used by boats to transport people, animals and goods. The River Nile was also the source of ancient Egypt's fertile soil. Egypt was 'the gift of the Nile' because without it the civilization could not have survived. Modern Egypt is still based around the river, which flows from the heart of Africa to the Mediterranean Sea.

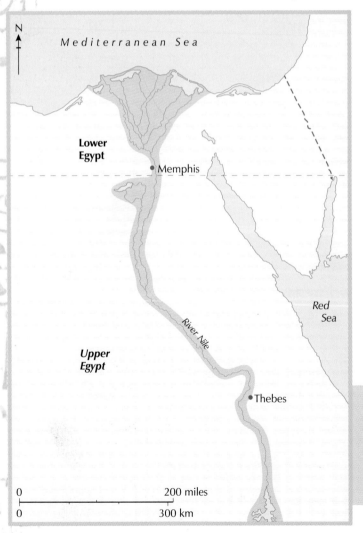

This map shows the location of the River Nile in Egypt and the area affected by the annual flood.

Ancient Egyptian Women

Ruth Manning

www.heinemann.co.uk/library

Visit our website to find out more information about **Heinemann Library** books.

To order:

☎ Phone 44 (0) 1865 888066

🖹 Send a fax to 44 (0) 1865 314091

💻 Visit the Heinemann Bookshop at www.heinemann.co.uk/library to browse our catalogue and order online.

First published in Great Britain by Heinemann Library, Halley Court, Jordan Hill, Oxford OX2 8EJ, part of Harcourt Education Ltd. Heinemann is a registered trademark of Harcourt Education Ltd.

© Harcourt Education Ltd 2002
First published in paperback in 2003
The moral right of the proprietor has been asserted.

Editorial: Nick Hunter and Jennifer Tubbs
Design: Jo Hinton-Malivoire and Tinstar Design (www.tinstar.co.uk)
Illustrations: Art Construction
Picture Research: Maria Joannou and Virginia Stroud-Lewis
Production: Viv Hichens

Originated by Ambassador Litho Ltd
Printed in China by Wing King Tong

ISBN 0 431 14582 2 (hardback)
06 05 04 03 02
10 9 8 7 6 5 4 3 2 1

ISBN 0 431 14587 3 (paperback)
06 05 04 03
10 9 8 7 6 5 4 3 2 1

British Library Cataloguing in Publication Data
Manning, Ruth
    Ancient Egyptian Women. – (People in the past)
    305.4'0932

Acknowledgements
The publishers would like to thank the following for permission to reproduce photographs: AKG London p. **27**, / Francois Guernet p. **37**, /Erich Lessing pp.**15**, **21**, **24**, **29**, **36**, /Rabatti-Domingie pp.**18**, **20**; Ancient Art and Architecture Collection pp. **6**, **12**, **13**, **17**, **26**, **32**, **35**, **41**, /Mary Jelliffe p.**28**; /R. Sheridan p. **38**; Bridgeman Art Library/Oriental Museum Durham University p. **8**; Philip Cooke/Magnet Harlequin p. **39**; CM Dixon p. **22**; Peter Evans p. **5**; Manchester Museum pp. **42**, **43**; Michael Holford pp. **10**, **14**, **19**, **30**; Scala Art Resource p. **40**; Werner Forman Archive p. **25**.

Cover photograph of Queen Nefertiti reproduced with permission of Photo Archive.

The publishers would like to thank Dr Christina Riggs for her assistance in the preparation of this book.

Every effort has been made to contact copyright holders of any material reproduced in this book. Any omissions will be rectified in subsequent printings if notice is given to the publishers.

The famous pyramids were built as tombs for the pharaohs (kings) of Egypt. Their queens were buried in smaller pyramids beside them.

Women of the Nile

This book looks at what we know about women in ancient Egyptian society. It looks at the family lives of Egyptian women, from their childhood until the time they married and had children of their own. It also examines what the wives and mothers of Egypt did during the day, whether they stayed at home or went out to work. You will find out about the clothes women wore, as well as their jewellery and make-up. Women also had an important part to play in ancient Egyptian religion and some, like Queen Hatshepsut, became powerful enough to rule the whole country.

Three thousand years of history

The beginning of ancient Egyptian history is usually dated to about 3000 BC. There are several reasons why this date is used: it was when Egypt became one land, rather than two separate kingdoms, the first pharaoh (Egyptian king) ruled the country, the first specially-built tombs were made and the first **hieroglyphs** were used for writing. Of course, much happened in Egypt before 3000 BC, but it was from this date onwards that the civilization of ancient Egypt began to flourish. For the next 3000 years Egypt was ruled by pharaohs until, in 30 BC, the last of them died, and Egypt became part of the Roman Empire.

Women in ancient Egyptian society

There are many ways for us to find out about life in ancient Egypt. Wealthy Egyptians built ornate tombs, such as the tomb of the young pharaoh Tutankhamen who died in 1323 BC. These tombs were filled with all the things that the dead person would need in the **afterlife**. These included models of things like food. There were also miniature models of people, for example servants, who would assist the dead person in the afterlife.

Models in the tombs of the poor were very crude, but those left by the rich were made of fine materials. The tomb walls were often lined with paintings, and **hieroglyphic** writing which tells us about the people of ancient Egypt.

This painting shows the Pharaoh Ramses III embracing the goddess Isis. We can get some idea of what wealthy women looked like from the picture of the goddess. Hieroglyphics can be seen behind the two figures.

Owning property

One way in which the women of ancient Egypt had more rights than women in many other ancient **civilizations** was in owning property. When a parent died, his or her property was normally divided equally between all their children. A wife also controlled a third of any property she owned with her husband. We know of at least one woman, called Naunakhte, who barred four of her eight children from inheriting her property because they had not looked after her in her old age.

Evidence from tombs

Only the richest and most powerful people in Egypt could afford to build these massive tombs for themselves. Most of the rulers and important government officials were men. **Archaeologists** have discovered that most of the tombs were built for men as well. Although they have found models and paintings of women in the tombs, archaeologists are not always sure whether these really tell us what Egyptian women were actually like – they may just show what men ideally wanted women to be. For example, most of the pictures are of young women, even if they show the tomb-owner's mother. There are plenty of pictures of old men, but very few of old women.

We do know that men and women were expected to play very different roles in ancient Egyptian society. For the most part, men governed the country while even the richest women looked after the house, the children and the servants. However, women were considered equal to their husbands in many things. They could take a case to court, run a business or serve as **priestesses** in the temples of Egypt.

Most of the evidence that has been found is about the lives of women from rich and powerful families. It is much more difficult to find out about ordinary women. They would have had few chances to own property, or to be buried in a tomb decorated with scenes from their lives.

Girls in ancient Egypt

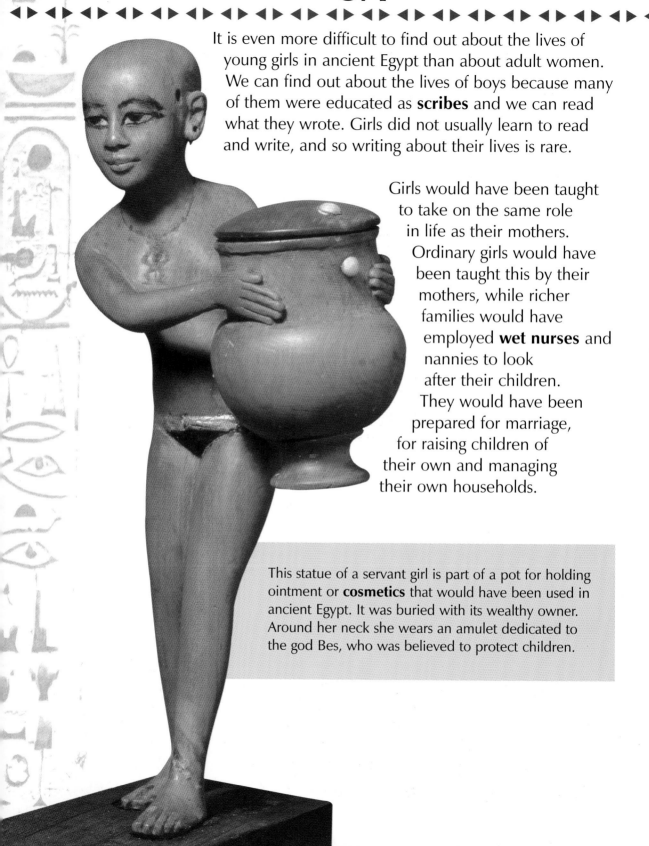

It is even more difficult to find out about the lives of young girls in ancient Egypt than about adult women. We can find out about the lives of boys because many of them were educated as **scribes** and we can read what they wrote. Girls did not usually learn to read and write, and so writing about their lives is rare.

Girls would have been taught to take on the same role in life as their mothers. Ordinary girls would have been taught this by their mothers, while richer families would have employed **wet nurses** and nannies to look after their children. They would have been prepared for marriage, for raising children of their own and managing their own households.

This statue of a servant girl is part of a pot for holding ointment or **cosmetics** that would have been used in ancient Egypt. It was buried with its wealthy owner. Around her neck she wears an amulet dedicated to the god Bes, who was believed to protect children.

Moving out

Egyptian girls would often have been married in their early teenage years. At this time, a girl would have left her parents' home and moved to the house of her husband. We also know that some girls left their family homes even though they were not married. They probably moved to the home of a wealthy family to work as servants.

Training to run the household

Girls would also have been trained to run a household. In wealthy families, this would have involved managing a team of servants. In ordinary homes, girls would have helped their mothers with the cooking, cleaning and other tasks needed to keep the house running. They may also have looked after younger children.

Getting dressed?

Children are normally shown naked in Egyptian tomb paintings. This may have been the artists' way of distinguishing children from adults, who are usually shown clothed. However, in the hot, dry land of Egypt, it seems likely that they often did not wear any clothes during the summer. Nudity was not considered unusual in ancient Egypt. If girls did wear clothes to protect them from the sun or to keep them warm in winter, they would have been very simple garments made of **linen.** Adults wore more ornate clothes for parties and formal occasions, such as religious ceremonies.

Girls' hairstyles

Statues and tomb paintings tell us about girls' hairstyles. Children of both sexes would normally have had all their hair shaved off apart from a small area at the side of the head. This was called a sidelock, and it shows that the girl is still a child. The statue on the opposite page may once have had a sidelock, all that can be seen today is a hole where it might have been attached. It does, however, show the girl's shaved head. Royal children may have worn a combination of **wig** and sidelock even when they were grown up. This showed that they were adults, but still the children of the pharaoh.

Education of girls and women

Although ancient Egyptian women certainly had more rights than women in many other ancient societies, it is very difficult for us to find out if women had the chance to learn to read and write. Boys in wealthy families would have been educated to become **scribes** and work in the government of Egypt. Women were not usually involved in government, and so the Egyptians didn't believe that they needed to read and write.

Boys were normally taught at home by their fathers, or in schools attached to the temples of Egypt. The daughters of wealthy families may have been educated alongside their brothers – it is very difficult to know for sure. Mothers who had learned the complex systems of Egyptian writing probably passed these skills on to their own daughters.

This is a statue of a nobleman and his wife. It was made in about 1450 BC. Many noblemen could read and write. It seems likely that their wives had enough education to help them in managing a large home and a team of servants.

Looking for clues

One of the problems is that there are no letters or other forms of writing that we know were definitely written by women. There are letters addressed to women, such as the writings of husbands who were away from home on official business, but the educated servants or sons of the house would probably have read these out loud to their mistresses. Without evidence of women's own writing, we can not know how many of them were educated. Tomb paintings have been discovered which show scribes' tools under the chairs that female figures are sitting on, but **archaeologists** believe that these tools belonged to their husbands.

Women as scribes

All the tomb paintings and models that archaeologists have found show male scribes. However, some people believe that women could have been a part of the most important Egyptian profession. The goddess of writing was Seshat, who was always shown as a woman. Her name is written by adding a feminine ending ('-at') to the word for 'scribe' or 'writing' ('sesh').

Managing the house

Wives were expected to manage the household. For the poor, the household would have been quite small. Wealthy women however may well have needed some knowledge of writing and maths in order to manage many servants, and the household accounts. Women sometimes set up businesses, for example trading in cloth. This is another area where understanding maths would have been important.

All the clues we have about the education of Egyptian girls and women are found in the possessions and images of wealthy women, whose fathers and husbands would have been part of the ruling class. We can be almost certain that few if any, poorer women would have had the opportunity to learn. Their time would have been spent looking after their families and houses.

Marriage

There was no religious marriage ceremony in ancient Egypt. It seems that men and women set up home together, and were then listed as 'married'. A register of people living at the workers' village of Deir el-Medina, near the Valley of the Kings, lists couples and families. Marriages were probably arranged between families. Fathers 'gave' their daughters to a suitable husband, who in return handed over a gift to his new wife. In some cases, a legal document was drawn up. This was really to protect each partner's property if the marriage broke up. The document would have been kept at the local temple, or another secure building.

Women certainly married when they were young. It was not unusual for girls in ancient Egypt to marry at the age of twelve. This was partly because the life expectancy of women was lower than that of men. The sole purpose of a marriage for the Egyptians was to produce children. Egyptian medicine was advanced for its time, but giving birth was risky and many young wives died as a result of childbirth.

An extended family

Most men had only one wife, though a very small number of rich men could keep 'secondary' wives or **concubines**. A man's household often had an assortment of female relatives – unmarried sisters, aunts, daughters, his mother-in-law, mother and grandmother. Tomb paintings sometimes show men with more than one wife. This normally meant that the man's first wife had died and he had remarried.

This couple, Ramose and his wife, are shown together in the man's tomb. We know they were married or they would have been seated separately.

Goddess of motherhood

Hathor was the goddess of joy, beauty, love and marriage. She helped mothers and babies during childbirth. She was also linked to music, song and dance. Hathor was a sky-goddess, the daughter of Re, and was often pictured as a cow or with a cow's head. Many carved figures have been found near the shrines of Hathor. **Archaeologists** think they were left by couples asking the goddess for a child.

The pharaoh had the biggest family: he could have several wives, numerous children, nurses and female servants. We are not sure how royal wives were chosen. We do know that pharaohs often married their sisters. This was because the pharaoh was thought of as a god and it was important that he married someone of equal status.

Divorce

Men admired faithful wives and good mothers. Married women were expected to be loyal to their husbands. For a man to show interest in a married woman was thought wrong. **Divorce** was allowed, and divorced people could marry again. Childless marriages often ended in divorce. After the death of her husband, a **widow** could also marry again.

This is a painting of the goddess Hathor. Here she is shown with a human head. The Egyptians believed that when a child was born, seven Hathors would decide his or her future life.

Family life

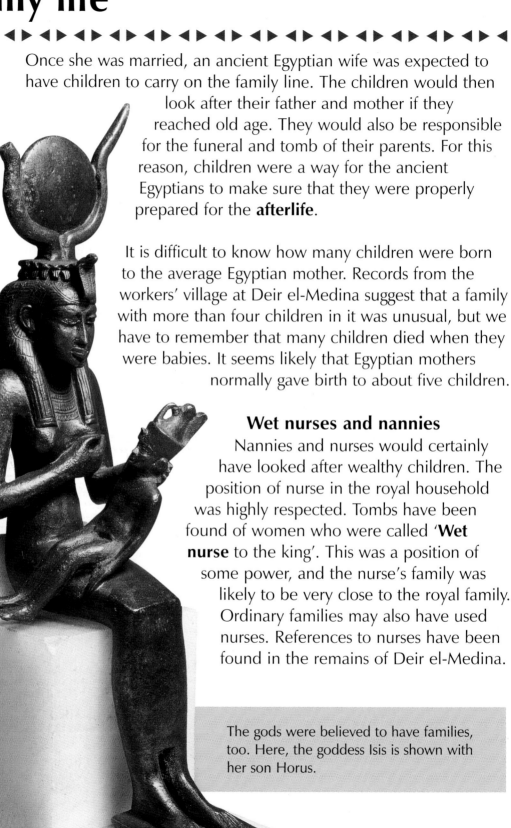

Once she was married, an ancient Egyptian wife was expected to have children to carry on the family line. The children would then look after their father and mother if they reached old age. They would also be responsible for the funeral and tomb of their parents. For this reason, children were a way for the ancient Egyptians to make sure that they were properly prepared for the **afterlife**.

It is difficult to know how many children were born to the average Egyptian mother. Records from the workers' village at Deir el-Medina suggest that a family with more than four children in it was unusual, but we have to remember that many children died when they were babies. It seems likely that Egyptian mothers normally gave birth to about five children.

Wet nurses and nannies

Nannies and nurses would certainly have looked after wealthy children. The position of nurse in the royal household was highly respected. Tombs have been found of women who were called '**Wet nurse** to the king'. This was a position of some power, and the nurse's family was likely to be very close to the royal family. Ordinary families may also have used nurses. References to nurses have been found in the remains of Deir el-Medina.

The gods were believed to have families, too. Here, the goddess Isis is shown with her son Horus.

Mother and son

A man held his mother in great esteem, so much so that in some tomb paintings a dead man's mother appears alongside his wife. Fathers were never given this honour. We can find out more about this from the writings of **scribes**, like Any, who wrote this about how a son should treat his mother: 'Double the food your mother gave you, support her as she supported you. She had a heavy load in you but she did not abandon you'. Another teacher of scribes told his pupils that: 'I shall make you love writing more than your mother'.

Adopting

The health of mothers and children was a major concern for the ancient Egyptians. Many **papyrus scrolls** have been found that look at the medical issues surrounding pregnancy and childbirth. Couples who were unable to have children, or whose children had died, could **adopt** children. This would ensure that they were cared for in their old age.

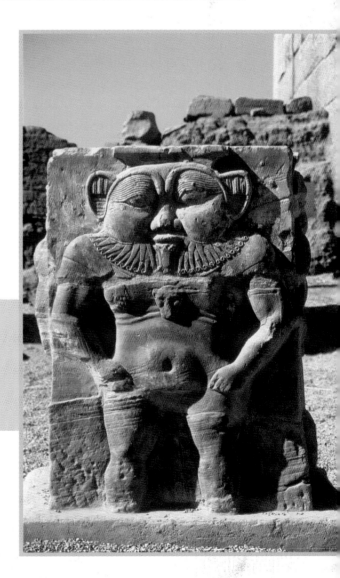

Bes was a protector of women and children. His ugly looks were designed to scare away demons from the household. This statue is in part of the temple of Hathor in Dandarah.

'Mistress of the household'

When a girl married, she became part of her husband's household. The families would carry wedding gifts and furniture through the streets from her parents' house. This was an important public display.

The Egyptians believed in large households. A typical family group might include the male head of the household, his wife and children, plus other unmarried or widowed female relatives such as sisters and aunts. Male relatives would have set up houses of their own. We know that the household of Hori, a soldier who lived in the town of Kahun, included Hori, his wife and son and also his mother and five of his sisters. They had probably become part of Hori's household when his father died.

Duties in the household

When she married, the new wife became 'mistress of the household'. This meant that while her husband went out to work, the young wife would manage the business of the household. This included care of the children, preparing food, cleaning the house and managing the servants and other members of the household.

Trouble and strife

One source that tells us a lot about ancient Egyptian family life is a set of letters written by the **scribe** Hekanakhte. He was sent to the **Nile Delta** on official business and wrote letters home to his family. Hekanakhte had five sons by his first wife, who had probably died. In one letter he tells his children that they should treat his second wife with more respect. The household also included his mother, at least two daughters and a maid.

Of course, in wealthy households servants would have done most of the work. Wives and other female members of the household may have had plenty of leisure time. Less well-off families, such as those of skilled craftsmen, would have had some servants, but the mistress of the household would have spent much of her time supervising them. In poorer households, the mistress herself would have done most of the work.

Doing business

As part of managing the household, women may have become involved in the world of business. In order to find food and other goods that they could not grow themselves, people would swap surpluses of food they had grown for other goods. Larger estates often employed merchants who would travel up and down the Nile trading goods for the estate. It is likely that the mistress of the household played some part in this trade, particularly in less wealthy households that could not afford to employ merchants.

Husbands and wives each had a different role to play in Egyptian life. This man would have left the running of his home to his wife while he went out to work.

Feeding the family

By far the largest part of an ancient Egyptian woman's day was probably spent preparing food for the family. Food had to be freshly prepared every day. Egyptian women had no refrigerators to keep the food cool and fresh in the hot Egyptian sun. A woman from each house had to collect water from the River Nile or, if the house was too far from the river, from a local well. This water was used to make the dough for bread, to boil meat and vegetables and to brew beer.

Everyday food

The mistress of an ordinary household would have been closely involved in preparing the daily meal. Other women in the house would also have helped out in preparing the meal. They would have cooked meat very rarely, but the River Nile would have provided plenty of fish. Many families grew their own vegetables on plots near their homes. The women of the house would have tended to these while the men went out to work.

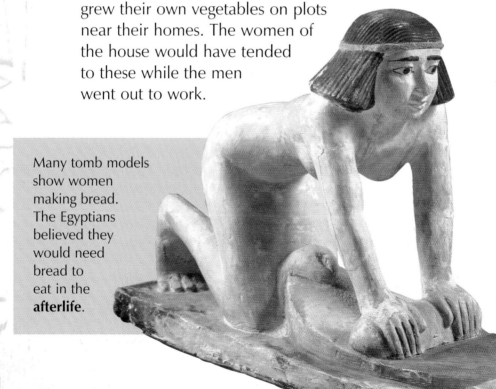

Many tomb models show women making bread. The Egyptians believed they would need bread to eat in the **afterlife**.

Daily bread

Bread was the most important part of the daily diet for rich and poor alike. We know how important bread was because tomb models show how it was made. Grain was ground on stones to turn it into flour. This would have been done by ordinary women or by servants. Because of the dry, dusty climate of Egypt, sand and grit would have become mixed in with the flour. **Archaeologists** have found the bodies of ancient Egyptian women and men with very worn teeth. They believe that this is a result of the grit in the bread that these people ate every day.

Egyptian banquets

The mistresses of larger households would have overseen the servants as they prepared the meal. The wealthy ate meat more often than ordinary people did because it was very expensive. Most Egyptians ate their main meal in the middle of the day when the sun was at its hottest, but wealthy families might also have held banquets with music and dancing in the evening. Tomb paintings tell us that single women all sat together at these banquets. Married couples are always shown together.

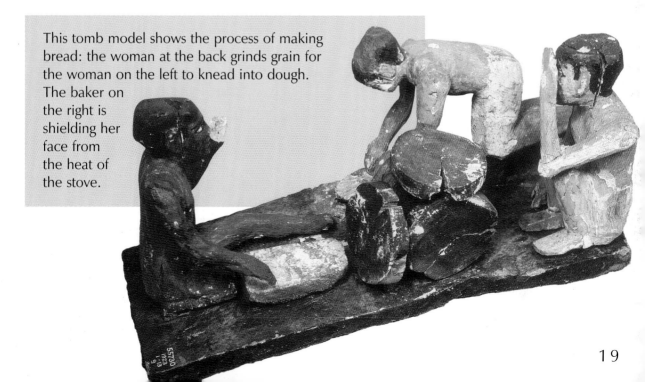

This tomb model shows the process of making bread: the woman at the back grinds grain for the woman on the left to knead into dough. The baker on the right is shielding her face from the heat of the stove.

Working outside the home

The main duties of an ancient Egyptian woman involved her household and family. Men were expected to work in the fields or helping to build the great **monuments** of Egypt. However, there were some women who went out to work.

Women as servants

Most ancient Egyptian households employed servants to help with cooking, cleaning and other household chores. Only the poorest households could not afford any servants at all. Most of the servants were women, particularly those who worked inside the house. Male servants would have worked outside in the fields.

Servants would usually have lived with the family they worked for. The largest estates even built special buildings to house their servants. These women were usually from the poorest families and unmarried, so they did not have households of their own to look after. In wealthy houses, some servants would have worked as maids, helping the mistress of the house to dress and make herself beautiful for banquets and other special occasions. Older women would have worked as nannies or **wet nurses**, they may have been **widows** who had experience of raising their own children.

Dancers and musicians

Many pictures have survived on the walls of tombs and temples that show women performing as musicians and dancers. Music was very important to the ancient

Servants would often have had to make food and beer, as shown by this tomb model that dates from the Old Kingdom.

Egyptians, and young women would often play tunes and songs for their own families. Professional troupes of musicians and dancers were linked to temples and royal households. This link to the rich and powerful is the main reason why pictures of dancers have survived as tomb paintings.

Troupes of musicians would perform at banquets, and were also an essential part of Egyptian funerals. In most areas of life, Egyptian men and women had very different places in society but music seems to have been one area where they worked together. Groups of musicians contained both men and women.

These musicians are carrying a double oboe, a lute and a harp. These are similar to instruments that are still played today.

Weaving workshops

Most clothes in ancient Egypt were made of **linen**. This was made from the **flax** that grew in the fertile fields beside the River Nile. Large estates had **weaving** workshops where the flax was woven into cloth. The servants who worked in the weaving workshop would have worked hard to make the fine linen that the wealthiest Egyptians wore. Older women would check the cloth to make sure that the quality was high.

Ladies of leisure

Most ancient Egyptian women would have had very little time for relaxing. They would have been kept busy running a household and looking after their families. Bread to feed the family had to be baked every day and, in the dry climate of ancient Egypt, the women must have been constantly trying to keep their houses free from dust.

Senet was a game for two players. It was played on a board of 30 squares. Each player tried to move their pieces, shaped like either a cone or a disc, across the board. This picture survives on a piece of **papyrus**.

Family outings

Boats appear everywhere in Egyptian thinking, and most Egyptians were never far from the River Nile. Many women took boat trips just for pleasure with their families, to visit friends in the next town, for a riverside picnic or to fish and hunt birds. The family would have sat under an awning or canopy at the back of the boat, which protected them from the fierce heat of the Egyptian sun. The pharaoh made the grandest of all river voyages, travelling in his royal barge with an escort of officials, servants and soldiers, as well as wives and other members of his family, to visit the towns and villages of Egypt.

Ordinary people sometimes enjoyed special meals, when they might eat meat. Music and dancing were important ways of relaxing for all ancient Egyptians both rich and poor. Girls and young women would sing and play for their families. We know very little about the songs they sang because, if they were ever written down, none of this written music has survived. Everyone would have celebrated around the local temple at the time of a religious festival.

Wealthy women, whose household chores were done by servants, would have had much more time for leisure. Many women from high-ranking families would spend this time working as **priestesses** for the goddess Hathor, or making music in temples.

Senet

Both men and women probably played the game of Senet. We do not know the rules, but boards and pieces for playing the game have been found in tombs. There are also paintings of husbands and wives playing the game. Instead of dice, players used **throwsticks** to decide how many moves they could make.

Clothes

Ancient Egyptian clothes were made from **linen**. Linen cloth was woven from the fibres of **flax**. The thinner the fibres were, the finer the linen. Wealthy Egyptians would have worn clothes made of linen that was much finer than the linen we have now, thousands of years later. Poor women would have worn clothes made of lower quality linen, woven from thicker and coarser fibres.

Ordinary women would probably have made these clothes themselves, along with the clothes for the rest of the family. The cloth would mostly have been made in workshops attached to large estates. Workers were often given cloth as part of their wages. Clothes would have been put together as simply as possible, without very much sewing.

Daily wear

For the everyday chores of running a busy household in the heat of Egypt, women would have worn the simplest clothes they could find. An Egyptian woman might have worn a lightweight wrap-around dress that would keep her cool, and not restrict her movement. Clothes that have survived were sewn down one side. They also had sleeves so the woman's shoulders were covered.

This tomb painting shows a husband and wife harvesting grain. People wanted to look their best for the afterlife so they are shown in their best clothes – even though they are working in the fields.

Clothing in art

Many tomb models of Egyptian women show them wearing tight linen dresses that are supported by straps over the shoulders. It would be easy for us to make the mistake of thinking that these dresses were worn every day. The dresses are so tight that it is hard to imagine anyone wearing them while cooking or doing chores! The artists were keen to show women as beautiful and able to bear children. No dresses like this have been found by **archaeologists**. Art from the later centuries of ancient Egypt gives a more realistic idea of women's clothing, showing more loose-fitting garments.

Most Egyptian women would not have worn shoes. If they did, the shoes would have been the same as the sandals that men wore. These would have been made of reeds or leather.

Evening wear

While linen was ideal for everyday wear in the hot Egyptian climate, it is very difficult to dye and could have seemed very plain when worn on a special occasion. Wealthy women, and those in the royal household, would have worn brighter clothes over their linen dresses. These were made of netting and decorated with colourful beads. We can find out about women's finest clothes because paintings in tombs usually show people in their best clothes in preparation for the **afterlife**.

This is a statue of Nofret, wife of Prince Rahotep. She lived around 2500 BC. This shows what the rich might have worn in the evening during the Old Kingdom of ancient Egypt.

Jewellery and wigs

Egyptian women loved jewellery, especially brightly coloured **semi-precious stones** such as blue lapis lazuli (brought from central Asia, around modern Afghanistan), purple amethyst, red cornelian and greenish-blue turquoise. Only the royal family and the very rich wore gold and silver jewellery, but even servant girls treasured stone or pottery beads strung on thin **copper** wire.

As you can see from this bracelet, Egyptian jewellery could be very ornate. It would also have been quite heavy to wear. It is made of lapis lazuli and other materials.

Jewels everywhere

Both men and women wore jewellery, on almost every part of their bodies. People wore religious charms for protection against evil, while jewellery was put into tombs for the dead person's use in the **afterlife**. Tombs contain hair bands, necklaces, earrings, neck-bands, collars, waist-girdles, bracelets for the upper arm and wrist, ankle-ornaments and rings for the fingers.

The jewellery a woman wore could be about more than just looking good. Necklaces have been found that included amulets, or lucky charms, to protect the wearer from the dangers of pregnancy and childbirth.

Wigs

Both men and women wore **wigs**. Many tomb paintings show people wearing them and **archaeologists** have even found wigs that have been preserved. For wealthy women, wigs might have been decorated with jewels. These ornate wigs would have shown other people that the wearer was important and wealthy.

Hairstyles

Hairstyles were an important part of looking good, and servants would have been trained to style the hair of their wealthy masters and mistresses. During the thousands of years of ancient Egyptian **civilization**, hairstyles seem to have changed quite a lot, although they did not change as quickly as modern fashions do today. In the Old Kingdom, wealthy women wore their hair short but the fashion changed and, during the Middle Kingdom, shoulder-length hair was popular. We should remember that these two periods were hundreds of years apart.

Different hairstyles may have told people about a woman's place in society. Girls and boys usually wore their hair short with a longer plait, or sidelock, falling down the side of the head. There were also different styles for married and unmarried women, and for maidservants. This tells us how important hairstyles were to women in ancient Egypt.

This is a bust of one of the wives of the pharaoh Amenhotep III. The head is made of ebony but the wig is made of canvas.

Cosmetics and beauty

The paintings and models that have survived since the time of the ancient Egyptians tell us a lot about their idea of beauty. As the pictures throughout this book show, the Egyptians liked to look their best in the images that filled their tombs. Paintings of rich Egyptian women show them with paler skin than their husbands. This shows us that men worked outside in the sun. It was probably thought unfeminine for a woman to spend too much time in the sun. Pale skin became fashionable.

Rich women went to a lot of trouble to make themselves look elegant. With the help of servants, they arranged their hair in ringlets and curls. They rubbed cleansing creams and oil into their skins, and wore perfume to make sure they smelled nice. Perfumes were made from flowers, sweet-smelling woods and spices soaked in oils. **Cosmetics** helped to keep off flies and other troublesome insects, and helped to protect the skin from the fierce sun.

Cosmetic boxes found in tombs contain make-up tools. There are tweezers for plucking unwanted hairs and make-up sticks for putting on eye make-up. Both men and women wore oily black eye paint called 'kohl'. They also put on eye paint made from grey galena (rock containing lead) and green copper oxide. Red **ochre** mixed with fat made a reddish make-up for the cheeks and lips. Egyptians used the reddish colouring **henna** to dye their hair (and to colour the soles of their feet and the palms of their hands).

In Egyptian tomb paintings, the eyes of the women and men pictured are covered with heavy make-up. This is a picture of the goddess Isis.

Incense cones

Pictures of women at banquets show them with what look like cones on their heads. These cones would probably have contained a greasy mixture of **incense**. As the evening went on, the grease would melt and the incense would ooze out of the cone and across the woman's head. This would have given off a sweet smell, but it must have been very messy! None of these cones has survived so we will never find out exactly how this perfume worked.

Mirrors

Egyptian mirrors were not made of glass; they were made of polished metal. **Archaeologists** have found mirrors that were used by the ancient Egyptians. They must have used the mirrors to apply their make-up correctly. As with many other areas of women's lives, we know lots about the make-up and beauty of the rich and fashionable. We know little about poorer people, but they would not have dressed up and adorned themselves in the same way as the wealthy.

This mirror is made of bronze. The handle is very ornate and it would have been highly prized by the woman who owned it.

Women as goddesses

All the people of ancient Egypt had the same religion. Men and women believed in many different gods and goddesses, each of whom would protect them in different areas of their lives. Many Egyptian goddesses were just as important as gods were. They were often guardians, protecting Egyptian women from the dangers of childbirth and illness.

Probably the most important goddess was Isis. Egyptians believed that she had saved Osiris, the Lord of the **underworld**, and she became the goddess of healing. Isis became even more important when she was later worshipped across the Roman Empire, alongside the Romans' own gods.

Isis was not only revered for rescuing Osiris. She was also believed to be the mother of Horus, the god who was the ancestor of all the pharaohs in the long history of Egypt.

Isis and Osiris

One of the most important myths about the Egyptian gods was the story of Isis and Osiris. Osiris taught the Egyptian people to farm the land, and ruled over a golden age of peace and prosperity. He married his sister, Isis. Their brother Seth was so jealous that he tricked Osiris, sealed him in a box and threw it into the Nile.

Seth retrieved the body and hacked it into small pieces, which he scattered all over the world. Isis found the pieces and bandaged them back together with a combination of skill and magic. Osiris' bandaged body was the first **mummy**. The Egyptians worshipped Isis as a healer of the sick.

Hathor

The cow-headed goddess Hathor played an important part in women's lives. She was the goddess of love and protected women in their daily lives particularly from illness and death in childbirth. **Archaeologists** have found many carved figures around the temples dedicated to Hathor. Most of these **offerings** were made by women. Hathor was also associated with music – an important part of the lives of many women.

Other important goddesses were Nephthys, the sister of Isis, who helped to save Osiris, and their mother Nut, the sky goddess. These were very important figures in Egyptian religion. Taweret, the goddess of childbirth, was one of many goddesses to have the head of an animal. In her case, it was a hippopotamus, one of the many animals that lived by the River Nile. Statues and paintings have been found that show Taweret with such hippopotamus features.

Women and temples

The many gods and goddesses of ancient Egypt were worshipped in temples. These great buildings, which were often almost as big and imposing as the pyramids of Egypt, have been preserved by the dry Egyptian climate. They can tell us a lot about Egyptian religion, and the role of women in the ceremonies and worship of the Egyptian gods and goddesses. The part women played in religion fell into two main areas: **priestesses** and musicians.

Women as priestesses

Ordinary ancient Egyptians would probably never have seen the insides of temples. Temples were the homes of the gods, and the people who served the gods – the priests and priestesses. Most of these people were men, but there were also women who worked in the temples. Many of those who served the goddess Hathor were certainly women. Priestesses served in the temples of male gods, too.

This priestess, called Henutmehit, was **mummified** and buried in this coffin that was decorated with gold. Many priestesses were the wives of powerful government officials. They had servants to manage their homes, which gave them spare time to work at the temple.

The god's wife of Amen

The rulers of Egypt were thought of as gods. A royal princess or wife of the pharaoh might earn the title of the God's Wife of Amen. Amen was the most powerful Egyptian god and the position of God's Wife would have brought a lot of power. We do not know exactly what the God's Wife did, but in paintings she is shown to be almost as powerful as the pharaoh. Queen Hatshepsut held the title of God's Wife during her rise to power.

The job of these priestesses involved organizing the temple. They would have tended the statues of the gods and organized **offerings**. They would also have helped with the management of other activities connected with the temple, such as musicians and the servants who worked on the estates around the temple.

Priestesses of Hathor would probably have come from the most important families of Egypt. Their husbands would have been powerful officials in Egypt's government. Despite this, the most important priests were always men. This was because men were taught to read, so they could read the prayers and **rituals** associated with the goddess.

Making music

Music was an important part of Egyptian religion, and women would have served as musicians in the temples. Many tombs show women who were musicians in the temple and this was a prized job at all levels of society. Female musicians also played in the temples of male gods. Wives of male priests were often musicians in the same temples as their husbands. The most common instrument they played was the sistrum, a type of rattle that was particularly associated with the temples of Hathor.

Into the afterlife

Ancient Egyptians believed that when they died they would pass into the **afterlife**. Men and women thought they would share in the same afterlife, and husbands and wives often shared the same tombs. They believed that the afterlife would include all the best parts of their life on the banks of the Nile.

From mothers to mummies

Women from wealthy families would have been **mummified**, just like their husbands, in preparation for the afterlife. The mummified body of the dead person would have been wrapped in **linen** bandages and placed in a **coffin**. The insides of the body would have been put into a series of jars so that the body could be thoroughly dried out.

During the period of the New Kingdom, which lasted from about 1539 BC to 1075 BC, women's burials were accompanied by many of the same objects that have been found in men's tombs. Many of the models of people found in the tombs were *shabtis* – miniature figures placed in the tomb to do the woman's work in the afterlife. They might also have been given a Book of the Dead. This was a book specially made for the dead person that would guide them through the dangers of the afterlife. We know that some were made for women because the pictures in each book show the person it was written for.

Mourning the dead

Many tomb paintings show women mourning the death of an important person. Many of these women would have been the man's relatives. Women also worked as professional **mourners**. This could be linked to their work as **priestesses** and dancers. They were employed to grieve openly around the house while the dead person was being mummified, and to mourn at the tomb. To show that they were mourning, they would cast dust on their heads, wail, and shriek and wave their arms.

Tombs of women

Most of the tombs that **archaeologists** have discovered were shared by women and their husbands. Most of the paintings inside the tombs showed both men and women – although the man buried in the tomb is often at the centre of the paintings. Women are not shown as clearly, or are shown at the side of the pictures. The husband and wife are often shown as if they are being buried together although it is likely that they died at different times. Women in the paintings are often mourning the death of their husbands, even if they had actually died first. This was to show the respect that the wife had for her dead husband.

If a person had many mourners, it showed that they were rich and powerful. This picture of mourners wailing and waving their arms in a funeral procession is from the tomb of the **scribe** Ramose.

Royal women

Most people in ancient Egypt were only married to one person at any time. However, pharaohs could have many different wives. They might marry members of their own families. We know that the young pharaoh Tutankhamen married his half-sister Ankhesenamen. Pharaohs might also marry girls from Egypt's other wealthy and powerful families. Many of the royal wives were foreign princesses. These marriages helped to build alliances between the powerful Egyptian pharaohs and the surrounding countries.

Chief wife and mother

The two most important women in ancient Egypt were the pharaoh's chief wife and his mother. We know more about some of these queens than we do about others. Often they are shown alongside the pharaoh in paintings and statues, meaning that they were very important. The queen most often shown is Nefertiti, the chief wife of the pharaoh Akhenaten. The mother of the pharaoh was believed to be close to the gods because her son was a god himself.

Unlike most queens, Nefertiti is often shown alongside her husband Akhenaten. Together they tried to start a new religion worshipping a sun god called the Aten. This change did not last long, but Nefertiti is remembered as one of the most beautiful and powerful women in ancient Egypt.

This decoration showing Tutankhamen and his wife Ankhesenamen is on the back of the throne that was discovered in the pharaoh's tomb.

The harem

The chief wife and the mother of the pharaoh were powerful women in their own right. They would have been given large houses full of servants to tend to their every need. However, the other women and maidservants of the royal household were a bit like servants of the pharaoh, and his many less important wives lived in a cross between a palace and a hotel on his estate known as a harem. There were many harems in different parts of Egypt and they would have been run by officials of the pharaoh. We know of a plot that started in one harem during the reign of Ramses III. One of his wives, called Tiy, planned to kill the pharaoh and place her own son on the throne.

Valley of the Queens

The Valley of the Kings is well known as the burial place of around 80 notable Egyptians, all men. Less well known is the nearby valley where their wives were buried, known as the Valley of the Queens. Pharaohs were normally buried separately from their wives. The most important tomb that has been discovered in this valley is of Queen Nefertari, the first wife of the Pharaoh Ramses II. Just as in the Valley of the Kings, robbers stole many of the treasures of these tombs thousands of years ago.

Queens of Egypt

Almost all of the rulers of Egypt were men, but there was one remarkable woman ruler. Her name was Hatshepsut, and she died in about 1458 BC. She is remembered for ruling during a successful time in Egypt's history, which included many building projects, **military campaigns** and trading expeditions.

How Hatshepsut came to rule Egypt

Hatshepsut was the daughter of the Pharaoh Thutmose I. Her brother Thutmose II became pharaoh in about 1482 BC, and Hatshepsut became his chief queen. When this weak pharaoh died about 1472 BC, his son Thutmose III was too young to reign. So Hatshepsut took control. She had herself crowned pharaoh, wore king's robes and even a false beard. She built a magnificent temple at Deir el-Bahri, and a row of **relief** pictures there show the ships she sent to the Land of Punt, in north-east Africa (roughly where Sudan and Eritrea are today).

Egypt's first female pharaohs

Hatshepsut was not the first woman to rule Egypt. In the 2nd **dynasty** officials decided that a woman could rule and at the end of the 6th dynasty a woman succeeded to the throne. Between about 1760 BC and about 1756 BC, Sobekneferu ruled after the death of her brother, Amenemhet IV. We know little about her short reign, apart from the fact that it marked the end of the 12th dynasty, one of the most successful periods in Egypt's history.

Hatshepsut tried to convince people that she was the same as any other pharaoh. Here she is shown wearing a false beard.

Hatshepsut always ruled alongside her step-son and nephew Thutmose III until she died in about 1458 BC. Later in his reign, Thutmose tried to destroy all traces of the rule of Hatshepsut. This may have been because he hated the fact that Hatshepsut had not allowed him to rule. It may also have been to prevent another female ruler – by pretending that it had never happened before. References to Hatshepsut as the wife of Thutmose II were not removed.

Cleopatra

There were several Egyptian queens called Cleopatra, the most well known is Cleopatra VII who ruled between 51 BC and 30 BC. She was the last queen of Egypt. At this time, Egypt had been conquered by the armies of Alexander the Great, and Cleopatra was really part of a Greek ruling family called the Ptolemies. She ruled alongside her father and brother, both called Ptolemy. We know most about her because the Roman general, Julius Caesar was thought to be the father of her son, and she also had a relationship with another Roman – Mark Antony. He gave her military support on behalf of Rome, but the rulers of Rome did not like this. Antony and Cleopatra, two of history's most famous partners, committed suicide after being defeated by Antony's rival, Octavian, at the Battle of Actium. Egypt became a **province** of the Roman Empire in 30 BC.

This temple built by Hatshepsut is one of the most imposing buildings that survive from ancient Egypt.

A fair society for women?

This book has explored what women could do in ancient Egypt. We have looked at what their lives were like and their place in society. However, the attitudes of the ancient Egyptians towards women were very different to the ideas we have today. There were many things that Egyptian women were not allowed, or not expected to do.

Going out to work

Although there are tomb models and paintings of women at work, the types of work they did were restricted. Women could work outside the home as musicians and dancers, or as servants in wealthy homes. However, most of their work was done at home: making bread and preparing meals, spinning and weaving cloth (although this was sometimes done in workshops on large estates). Today, all jobs are open to men and women, but in ancient Egypt women never worked as farmers or builders. On the other hand, men could be weavers and work in a **granary**.

Writing was an important sign of status in ancient Egypt. Because few women could write, it was difficult for them to get involved in work outside the home and in the government of Egypt.

School and writing

In ancient Egypt, knowing how to write was a passport to wealth and power. The people who were taught to write and play a part in the government of Egypt were, as far as we know, all boys. Educated **scribes** counted the harvests, and calculated the taxes that were due to the pharaoh. This group of scribes enabled Egypt's rulers to have more control over their people than any **civilization** before them. Men always wielded this power.

The art of Egypt

The status of women is shown most clearly in the art of ancient Egypt. They are always shown to be less important than their husbands and sons. This tells us that, although Egyptian women had a clear place and a role to play in society, they were always thought of as less important members of that society. If we compare ancient Egypt to our own society, we can see that Egypt was not really a fair society for women.

Many of the pictures that survive of women show them as strong figures, but they are nearly always secondary to Egyptian men.

Finding out about ancient Egyptian women

Archaeologists have been trying to find out about ancient Egypt and its people for centuries. Until the beginning of the 19th century AD, people could only guess at the importance of the temples and tombs of ancient Egypt. **Mummies** had been discovered, but no one knew why the Egyptians had preserved dead bodies. They knew the symbols that made up **hieroglyphic** writing, but did not know how to read them.

In AD 1799, a stone was found that included the same **inscription** in three different types of writing: hieroglyphic and **demotic** forms of Egyptian writing and ancient Greek. It was named the Rosetta Stone. **Historians** could translate the Greek and work out from this what the **hieroglyphs** meant. The French historian who deciphered the Rosetta Stone was called Champollion. His discovery was the most important one ever made in the study of ancient Egypt.

Archaeologists could now learn more about Egyptian beliefs about life after death by reading the hieroglyphs in tombs. They could understand more about the thousands of mummies that had been found. Previously people believed that eating powdered mummy could be a cure for illnesses.

People have studied the mummies of ancient Egypt with the help of modern science. Scientific techniques can give us detailed information about how Egyptian women lived and died.

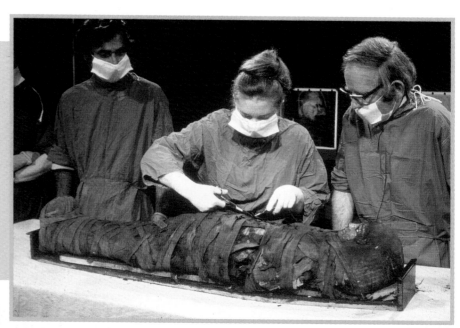

Mummy 1770 – a girl from ancient Egypt

One of the mummies that has been studied by archaeologists is of a young girl simply called 'Mummy 1770'. Researchers in Manchester studied this mummy of a fourteen-year-old girl in AD 1975. As each layer of the mummy was unwrapped, they found out more about the life of the girl. They discovered that she had died from a disease caused by a parasite. Both the girl's legs had been amputated by doctors, possibly in a final attempt to save her life. The researchers have been able to discover more about the diseases that affected Egyptian women from mummies like 'Mummy 1770', and the ways that Egyptian doctors could treat them. Modern medical techniques, like the use of X-rays and the study of body tissue, mean that scientists are finding out more and more about women and girls who lived in ancient Egypt.

Still much to learn

As a result of modern techniques like the ones used by archaeologists and scientists to examine 'Mummy 1770', we now know more than we have ever known before about the lives of women in ancient Egypt. There is still much for us to learn, but archaeologists hope that as they dig deeper into the traces left over the 3000 years that this amazing **civilization** lasted, they will be able to piece together even more of the remarkable story of ancient Egypt's women.

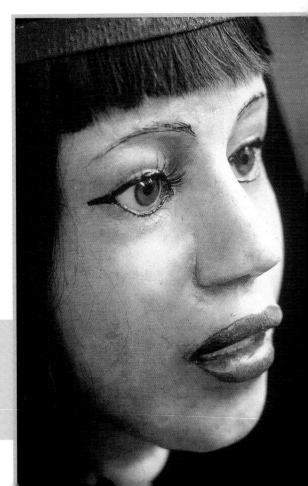

Studying the remains of Mummy 1770 has enabled scientists to make this model of her face. We can find out what ancient Egyptian women really looked like from such sources.

Timeline

◄► ◄► ◄► ◄► ◄► ◄► ◄► ◄► ◄► ◄► ◄► ◄► ◄► ◄► ◄► ◄► ◄► ◄

All dates are BC. Pharaohs' dates refer to reigns.

About 3000
King Menes, the first pharaoh, rules all Egypt.

2575 to 2130 Old Kingdom
Imhotep builds the first pyramid at Saqqarah. King Khufu builds the Great Pyramid at Giza.

1938 to 1600 Middle Kingdom
First schools in Egypt. City of Thebes becomes the capital.

1539 to 1075 New Kingdom
1472 to 1458 Reign of Queen Hatshepsut, alongside her step-son and nephew Thutmose III.

1353 to 1336
Reign of Akhenaten. His wife Nefertiti is one of the most famous Egyptian queens.

1335 to 1332
Reign of Smenkhkare. This may have been the name used by Nefertiti if she ruled after her husband died.

1333 to 1323
Tutankhamen rules Egypt.

1070 to 332
Libyan and Nubian kings rule Egypt. Assyrians invade Egypt. Persians also invade.

332
Egypt conquered by Alexander the Great. He makes Alexandria the capital. Greek kings known as Ptolemies rule Egypt. It covers the time from 332 until 30.

51 to 31
Reign of Cleopatra, Queen of Egypt. After her death, Egypt is ruled by Rome.

Sources and further reading

Sources

Ancient Egypt, David Silverman
(Judy Piatkus Ltd, 1997)

People of the Pharaohs, Hilary Wilson
(Michael O'Mara Books, 1997)

Women in Ancient Egypt, Fiona MacDonald
(Belitha Press, 1999)

Women in Ancient Egypt, Gay Robins
(British Museum Press, 1993)

Young Researcher: The Egyptians, Stuart Fleming
(Heinemann Educational, 1992)

Further reading

Ancient Egypt, Judith Crosner
(Hamlyn, 1992)

Explore History: Ancient Egypt, Jane Shuter
(Heinemann Library, 2001)

How Would You Survive as an Ancient Egyptian? Jacqueline Morley
(Franklin Watts, 1999)

Legacies of Ancient Egypt, Anita Ganeri
(Belitha Press, 1999)

Women in Ancient Egypt, Fiona MacDonald
(Belitha Press, 1999)

Glossary

▶◀▶ ◀▶ ◀▶ ◀▶ ◀▶ ◀▶ ◀▶ ◀▶ ◀▶ ◀▶ ◀▶ ◀▶ ◀▶ ◀▶ ◀▶ ◀▶ ◀

adopt/adoption when a couple bring up a child born to another mother as their own child

afterlife life after death

archaeologist person who finds out about the past by looking for the remains of buildings and other objects, often beneath the ground

civilization society with its own rules, and an advanced way of life

coffin box in which the body of a dead person is put

concubine woman who lived with a king but was not married to him

copper soft metal used by ancient peoples to make tools

cosmetics make-up; creams, paints, or scents used to make a person look, feel or smell nice

demotic simplified version of writing

divorce separation of a husband and wife by law

dynasty ruling family. The first Egyptian historian Manetho listed 30 dynasties of kings.

excavating digging into the ground by archaeologists to uncover the ruins of a building or a tomb

flax plant whose stalk fibres are used to make linen

granary storage place for grain

henna natural reddish dye used on the hair and body

hieroglyph picture that represents a sound, word or thing used in ancient Egyptian writing

hieroglyphics Egyptian picture-writing, the name means 'sacred writing' in Greek

historian someone who studies the past from writings, and writes about ancient peoples

incense substance which is burned or melted to give off a perfumed smell

inscription writing cut into stone or some other hard material

linen cloth made from the woven fibres of the flax plant

military campaigns organized sets of army manoeuvres to achieve a certain goal

monument building or statue built to remind people of a famous person or a famous event

mourner person grieving over a dead person, at a funeral and afterwards

mummify treat a dead body by drying it out and wrapping it in bandages

mummy body of a dead person specially treated to stop it decaying

Nile Delta area in northern Egypt where the River Nile meets the sea

ochre natural stain of a reddy-brown colour

offering gift or token made as a present to a god or goddess

papyrus scroll Egyptian book. Long strips of paper made from a reed called papyrus, were wrapped up in a roll around a stick.

priestess woman with special religious duties. In Egypt priestesses looked after temples.

province area in a country or empire

relief carving in stone where the picture stands out from the surface

ritual series of actions carried out in a set pattern during a ceremony

scribe person trained to write. In Egypt scribes wrote government records and wrote letters for other people.

semi-precious stones mineral which is used in jewellery, but is thought to be less valuable than a jewel

throwsticks part of a game that had the same function as a dice

underworld where dead people were thought to live, beneath the earth's surface

weaving intertwining thread to make cloth

wet nurse woman employed to care for another's child

widow woman whose husband has died

wig artificial hair

wildfowl birds like ducks that live in the wild and not as pets

Index